Cover and Title Page: Nathan Love

www.mheonline.com/readingwonders

Copyright © 2016 McGraw-Hill Education

All rights reserved. No part of this publication may be reproduced or distributed in any form or by any means, or stored in a database or retrieval system, without the prior written consent of McGraw-Hill Education, including, but not limited to, network storage or transmission or broadcast for distance learning.

Send all inquiries to:
McGraw-Hill Education
2 Penn Plaza
New York, NY 10121

ISBN: 978-0-02-130827-9
MHID: 0-02-130827-6

Printed in the United States of America

7 8 9 LMN 25 24 23

ELD
Companion Worktext

Program Authors

Diane August

Jana Echevarria

Josefina V. Tinajero

Unit 3

One of a Kind

The Big Idea
Why are individual qualities important? 2

Week 1 • Be Unique — 4

More Vocabulary 6
Shared Read The Inchworm's Tale Genre • Folktale 8
Respond to the Text 14
Write to Sources 16

Week 2 • Leadership — 18

More Vocabulary 20
Shared Read Jane's Discovery Genre • Historical Fiction 22
Respond to the Text 28
Write to Sources 30

Week 3 • Discoveries 32

More Vocabulary 34
Shared Read Earth and Its Neighbors   Genre • Expository Text 36
Respond to the Text 42
Write to Sources 44

Week 4 • New Ideas 46

More Vocabulary 48
Shared Read Bats Did It First   Genre • Expository Text 50
Respond to the Text 56
Write to Sources 58

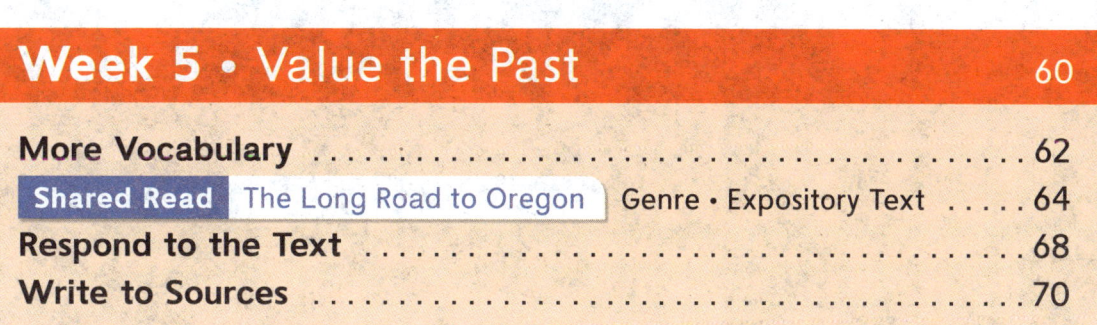

Week 5 • Value the Past 60

More Vocabulary 62
Shared Read The Long Road to Oregon   Genre • Expository Text 64
Respond to the Text 68
Write to Sources 70

One of a Kind

THE BIG IDEA

Why are individual qualities important?

TALK ABOUT IT

Weekly Concept Be Unique

? Essential Question
What makes different animals unique?

>> *Go Digital*

 What makes dolphins unique? Write things that make dolphins unique in the web. Describe how dolphins are different from other animals.

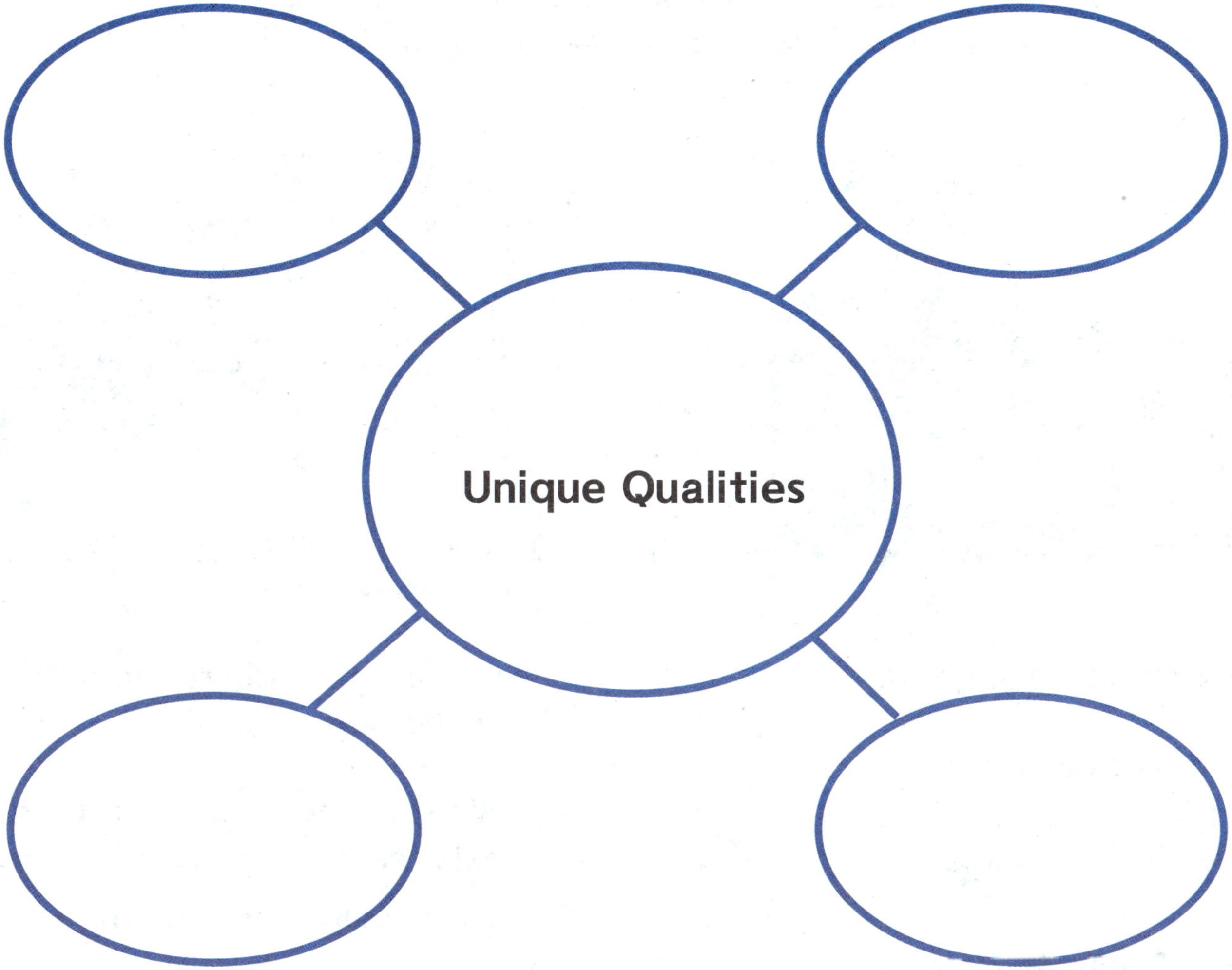

Unique Qualities

Discuss how a dolphin's unique qualities help it survive. Use the words from the chart. You can say:

A dolphin's _____ helps it _____.

A dolphin's _____ help it _____.

More Vocabulary

Look at the picture and read the word. Then read the sentences. Talk about the word with a partner. Write your own sentence.

exhausted

Ben is **exhausted** after the game.

What word means the same as *exhausted*?

sick   tired   small

When are you exhausted?

I feel exhausted when _____
_____
_____.

volunteered

The girls **volunteered** to build the house.

What words mean almost the same as *volunteer*?

ask to help   try to learn   want to play

When do you volunteer?

I volunteer when _____
_____
_____.

Words and Phrases: Homophones *week* and *weak*

week = seven days

We will visit Grandma this **week**.

weak = not strong

The old stairs are broken and **weak**.

Talk with a partner. Look at the pictures. Read the sentences. Write the word that completes the sentence.

Jen's birthday is next _____.

                    week   weak

The kitten is small and _____.

                    week   weak

Text Evidence

Shared Read — Genre • Folktale

1 Talk About It

Look at the picture. Read the title. Discuss what you see. Use these words.

children   rock   high   sky

Write about what you see.

The story is about _____

_____

_____.

Where are the children in the picture?

The children are _____

_____

_____.

Take notes as you read the story.

THE INCHWORM'S TALE

Essential Question

? What makes different animals unique?

Read about how one animal uses its special features to solve a problem.

8

One day long ago, Anant and his sister Anika went swimming. They swam all afternoon until they were **exhausted**. They felt very tired and fell asleep on a big, flat rock. Then something *surprising* happened. The rock began to grow. It grew until it reached the clouds.

Anant and Anika woke up high in the sky. They saw blue sky and big, white clouds. Anika felt dizzy. Anant looked for a way to climb down. He did not find a way down. Then Anika and Anant started to cry. They felt afraid.

Text Evidence

❶ Specific Vocabulary

Reread the first paragraph. *Surprising* means "unusual or not planned." What is surprising? Underline the sentence that tells you.

❷ Sentence Structure

Look at the second paragraph. Draw a box around the pronoun *he*. What noun does *he* refer to? Write the noun.

The pronoun he refers to _____
_____.

❸ Comprehension
Problem and Solution

What problem do the children have?

The children are _____
_____
_____.

Text Evidence

1 Specific Vocabulary

Reread the first paragraph. The word *searched* means "tried to find." Who searched for the children? Circle the words.

2 Sentence Structure

Reread the second paragraph. The word *finally* tells what happens last. Underline what happens last. What does Hawk do before he sees the children?

Before Hawk sees the children,

he _____

_____.

3 Comprehension
Problem and Solution

Reread the last paragraph. What is Hawk's problem?

Hawk wants to save _____

_____,

but _____.

The people at home in the village were worried. They searched everywhere for the children. The village chief was named Isha. Isha asked Hawk to help find the children. Hawk had strong eyes and strong wings.

Hawk agreed to help. He flew up into the sky and searched for the children. Finally, he saw the boy and girl on the rock. Hawk wanted to help the children. But Hawk could not carry them down the rock because they were too big.

Hawk returned to tell Isha what happened. Isha asked all the animals for help. Isha asked the animals to use their unique features to climb the tall rock. Several animals tried to climb the rock.

Mouse had strong teeth, but the teeth did not help her. She could not climb the rock.

Bear used his big claws to climb trees. But he was not able to climb the rock.

Mountain Lion had sharp and powerful claws. But the rock was slippery. Mountain Lion slid back down.

Finally, Inchworm spoke up in an **eager** way. "May I try, please? It's me, Too-Tock, the Inchworm!"

Text Evidence

1 Comprehension
Problem and Solution

Reread the first paragraph. How does Isha want to help the children? Underline the sentence that tells you.

2 Talk About It

Why is Mountain Lion not able to climb the rock?

Mountain Lion has _____,

but _____

_____.

3 Specific Vocabulary

Look at the last paragraph. The word *eager* means "excited to do something." Circle the name of the eager character.

Text Evidence

1 **Comprehension**
Problem and Solution

Look at the first paragraph. What is the plan to help the children? Underline the two sentences that tell you.

2 **Sentence Structure** ACT

Reread the second sentence in paragraph two. Circle the pronoun *they*. Who does *they* refer to? Circle the names of the characters.

3 **Talk About It**

Look back at page 11. Compare Inchworm with Bear. Write your ideas. Cite text evidence.

Bear has _____, but

he cannot _____.

Inchworm is a _____,

and she can _____.

Inchworm was a skillful climber. And she wanted to help the children. She and Hawk made a plan. Hawk **volunteered** to carry Inchworm to the top of the big rock. Then Inchworm would lead the children down. Isha liked this plan.

So Hawk carefully picked up Inchworm with his beak. Together they flew to the top of the rock. Inchworm planned the trip down during the flight. The children were waiting.

Inch by inch, Inchworm led the children down the big rock. Inchworm moved very carefully. The climb down to the village took a week. Hawk brought food to the children every day.

Finally, Inchworm, Anant, and Anika reached the bottom. Everyone cheered. Inchworm was a hero. It was a wonderful, glorious day.

Isha was happy. He said, "I rename the big rock Too-Tock-Awn-oo-Lah, after the brave inchworm."

Make Connections

? What unique feature does Inchworm have? How does it help? **ESSENTIAL QUESTION**

What do your special features help you do? **TEXT TO SELF**

Text Evidence

1 Sentence Structure

Look at the first sentence in the second paragraph. Circle the commas. Underline each character's name.

2 Specific Vocabulary

Look at the last sentence in the second paragraph. Which word helps you know meaning of *glorious*? Underline the word.

COLLABORATE

3 Talk About It

Discuss what happens after Inchworm goes to the top of the rock. Take notes. Then paraphrase the events in this part of the story. Write your ideas.

_____
_____
_____

Respond to the Text

 **Partner Discussion** Work with a partner. Read the questions about "The Inchworm's Tale." Show where you found text evidence. Write the page numbers. Discuss what you learned.

How is Inchworm different from other animals?

Inchworm is good at _____. Page(s): _____

Inchworm can fit into _____. Page(s): _____

Inchworm moves _____. Page(s): _____

How do Inchworm and Hawk help the children?

The children are on _____. Page(s): _____

Hawk and Inchworm fly to _____. Page(s): _____

Then Inchworm leads _____. Page(s): _____

 **Group Discussion** Present your answers to the group. Cite text evidence for your ideas. Listen to and discuss the group's opinions.

 **Write** Work with a partner. Look at your notes about "The Inchworm's Tale." Write your answer to the Essential Question. Use text evidence to support your answer. Use vocabulary words in your writing.

> **How do Inchworm's special features help her solve the problem?**
>
> The children need help because _____.
>
> Inchworm volunteers to _____.
>
> She is good at _____ and moves very _____.
>
> Inchworm uses her special features to _____
>
> _____
>
> _____.

Share Writing Present your writing to the class. Discuss their opinions. Talk about their ideas. Explain why you agree or disagree with their ideas. You can say:

I agree with _____.

That's a good comment, but _____.

Write to Sources

Nya

Take Notes About the Text I took notes about the story to respond to the prompt: *Add a paragraph to the end of the story. Tell what the children say to Inchworm.*

pages 8–13

Anant and Anika cannot find a way down the rock.

↓

The children cry.

↓

Inchworm leads the children down the rock.

↓

Everyone cheers. Inchworm is a hero.

Write About the Text My descriptive paragraph tells what the children say to Inchworm.

Student Model: *Narrative Text*

Anant and Anika thanked Inchworm. Inchworm took the children down the rock.

"You helped us," Anika said. "How can we thank you?"

Inchworm said, "I am hungry." She wanted to eat some leaves.

The children found some leaves and gave them to Inchworm. Inchworm smiled. Inchworm ate the leaves.

TALK ABOUT IT

Text Evidence
Draw a box around the sentence that tells how Inchworm helped the children. What action does the sentence show?

Grammar
Underline the past tense verb in the first sentence. Why does Nya use past-tense verbs in the story?

Condense Ideas
Circle the last two sentences about Inchworm. How can you use the word *and* to condense the sentences?

Your Turn

Add another paragraph to the story. Tell what happens when Mouse tries to climb the rock.

» Go Digital
Write your response online. Use your editing checklist.

17

TALK ABOUT IT

Weekly Concept Leadership

? Essential Question
How can one person change the way you think?

>> *Go Digital*

 Jackie Robinson was a leader. What does a leader do? Write qualities of good leaders in the web. Describe how leaders change the way people think.

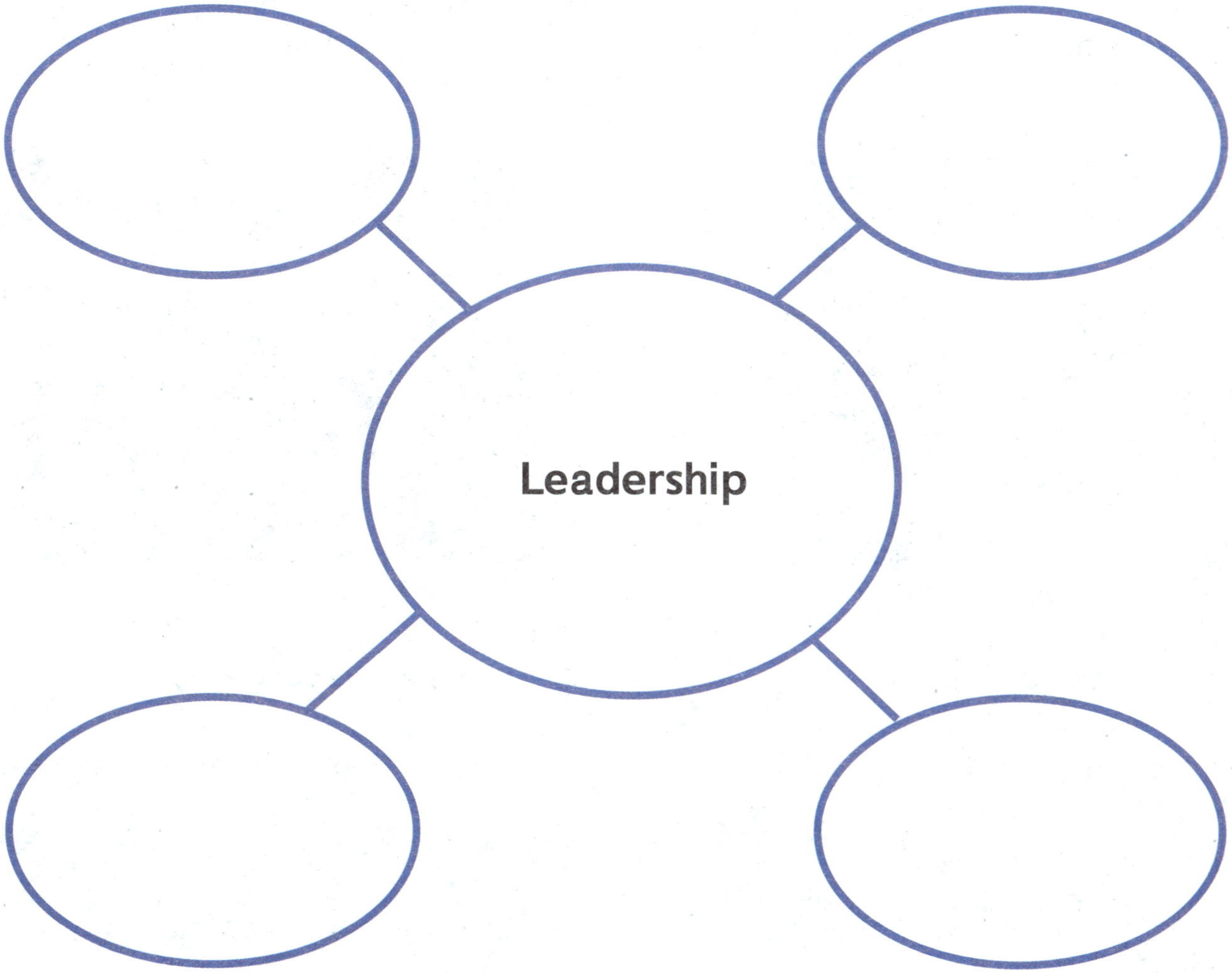

Leadership

Discuss the qualities of a good leader. Use the words from the chart. You can say:

A good leader is _____ and _____.

These qualities change how people _____.

More Vocabulary

 Look at the picture and read the word. Then read the sentences. Talk about the word with a partner. Write your own sentence.

belonged to

The two fish **belonged to** Eve.

What words mean the same as *belonged to*?

owned by   looked at

What belongs to you?

The _____

belongs to me.

favorite

The boy's **favorite** color is blue.

Complete the sentence. Write the word.

Pam's _____ color is red.

What is your favorite color?

My favorite color is _____

_____

_____ .

Words and Phrases: Contractions

A contraction is a short form of two words.

I am = *I'm*

I am reading a book.

I'm reading a book.

An apostrophe (') stands for the missing letters.

I will = *I'll*

I will eat my lunch.

I'll eat my lunch.

 Talk with a partner. Look at the pictures. Read the sentences. Write the contraction for the underlined words.

I am walking my dog.

_____ walking my dog.

I will wash the dishes.

_____ wash the dishes.

Text Evidence

Shared Read | Genre • Historical Fiction

1 Talk About It

Look at the picture. Read the title. Discuss what you see. Use these words.

girl   Jane   country   angry

Write about what you see.

The story is about _____

_____.

Where is Jane?

Jane is in the _____

_____.

How does Jane feel in the picture?

Jane looks _____

_____.

Take notes as you read the story.

Jane's Discovery

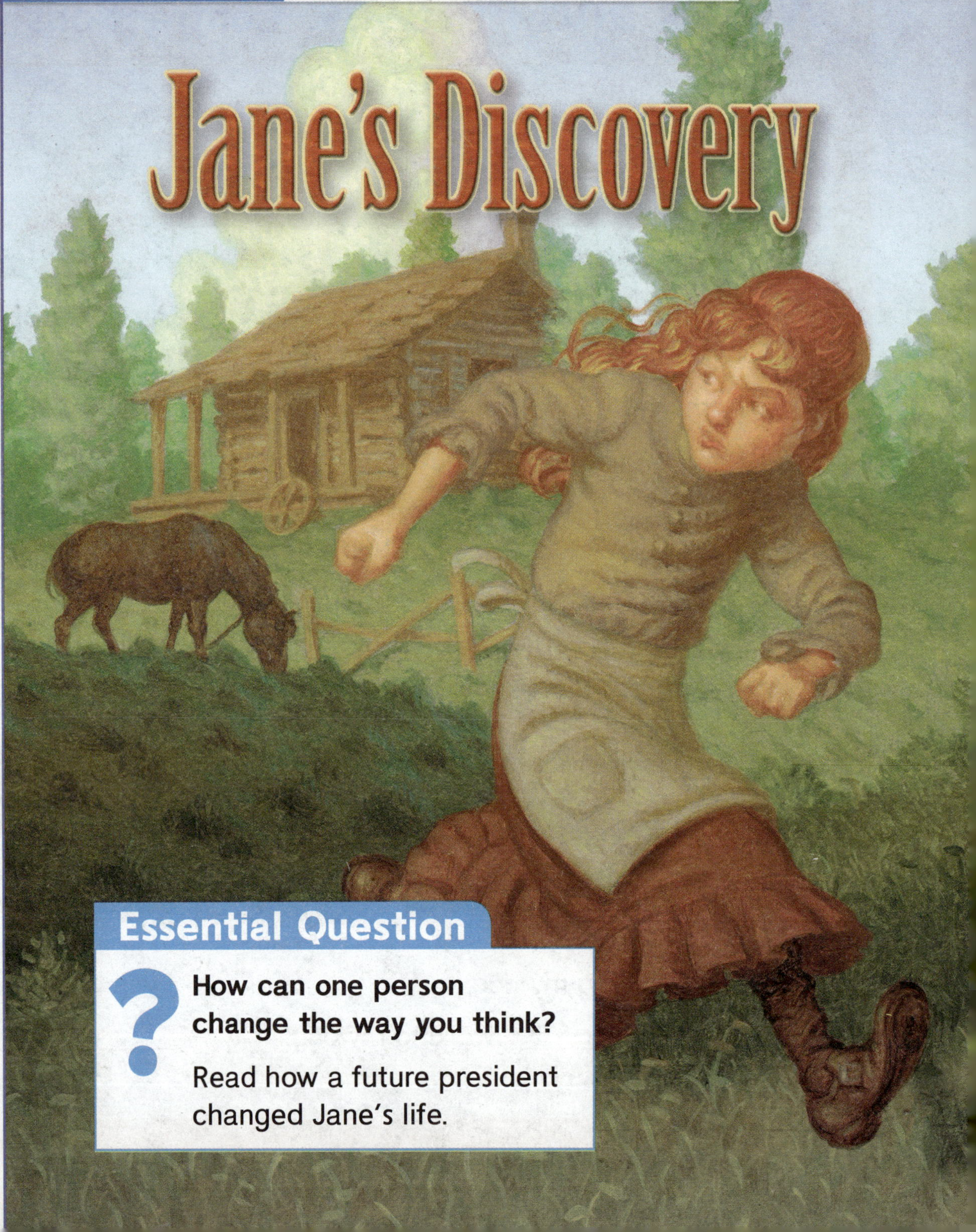

Essential Question

How can one person change the way you think?

Read how a future president changed Jane's life.

Jane ran out of her cabin, and she raced toward the woods. It was September 1825. Her parents wanted Jane to go to school and learn how to read. But Jane wanted to help on the farm. So Jane told her parents, "No!"

Jane ran for a long time. Running helped her think. Jane **dashed** around a tree and was not paying attention. As a result, she tripped and fell over two long legs.

The legs **belonged to** her neighbor, Abe Lincoln. Abe was reading a book under a tree. He smiled and helped Jane up.

Text Evidence

❶ Sentence Structure

Read the third sentence in the first paragraph. What do Jane's parents want her to do? Underline the two actions. What word connects the actions? Circle the word.

❷ Specific Vocabulary

Read the second paragraph. *Dashed* means "moved quickly." What is another word in the paragraph that means the same as *dashed*? Underline the word.

❸ Comprehension
Cause and Effect

Read the last two sentences in the second paragraph. What causes Jane to trip over two legs?

Jane trips because _____

_____

_____.

Text Evidence

1 Specific Vocabulary

Look at the word *recognized*. The word *recognize* means "know who someone is." Who does Jane recognize?

Jane recognizes _____.

2 Sentence Structure

Reread the second paragraph. Circle the punctuation marks that show someone is speaking. Then underline the name of the speaker.

3 Comprehension
Cause and Effect

Read what Jane says. Circle the word *because*. It shows why something happens. Why is Jane upset?

Jane is upset because _____

_____

_____.

Jane **recognized** Abe. She knew two things about Abe. He was a hard worker, and he also liked to read. He read all the time.

Abe asked, "Why are you running so fast?"

Jane said, "I'm upset because my parents want me to learn to read. I do not want to learn to read!"

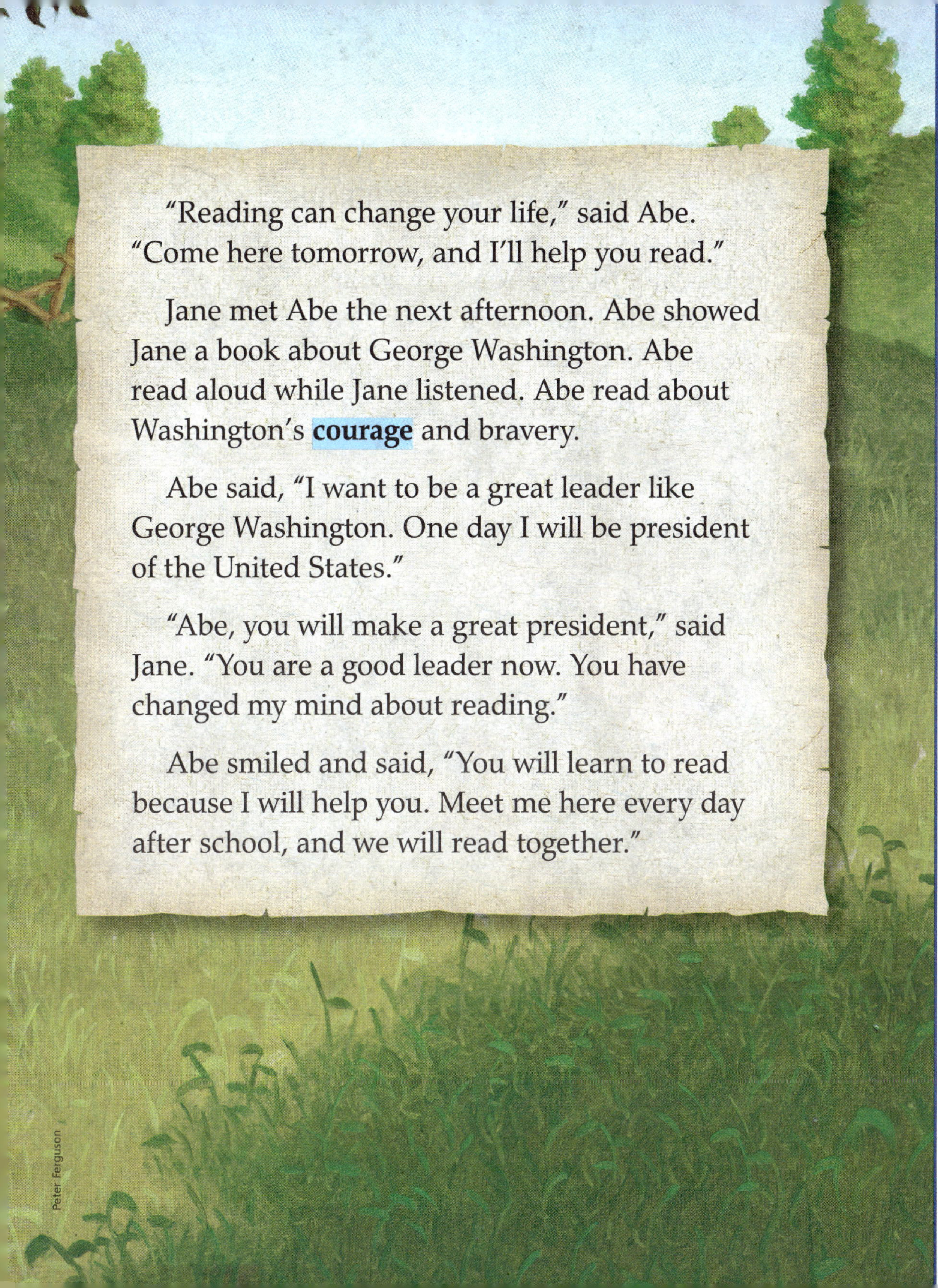

"Reading can change your life," said Abe. "Come here tomorrow, and I'll help you read."

Jane met Abe the next afternoon. Abe showed Jane a book about George Washington. Abe read aloud while Jane listened. Abe read about Washington's **courage** and bravery.

Abe said, "I want to be a great leader like George Washington. One day I will be president of the United States."

"Abe, you will make a great president," said Jane. "You are a good leader now. You have changed my mind about reading."

Abe smiled and said, "You will learn to read because I will help you. Meet me here every day after school, and we will read together."

Text Evidence

❶ Sentence Structure
Reread the third sentence of the second paragraph. Circle the word *while*. *While* shows that two things happen at the same time. Underline the two things that happen in this sentence.

❷ Specific Vocabulary
Reread the sentence with the word *courage*. Which word in the sentence means the same as *courage*? Circle the word.

❸ Talk About It
Why does Jane think Abe will make a great president? Write your ideas. Cite text evidence.

Abe is _____

_____

_____.

25

Text Evidence

1 Specific Vocabulary ACT

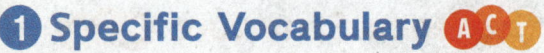

Look at the first sentence. The word *nervous* means "anxious or worried." Circle words that tell you what Jane is nervous about.

2 Comprehension

Cause and Effect

Reread the paragraph. Circle the signal word *as a result*. It signals an effect. What happens when Abe and Jane read together every day? Write the effect.

Effect: Jane ______________________

______________________________.

3 Sentence Structure ACT

Reread the last sentence. An adjective describes a noun. What adjective describes the noun *book*? Circle the adjective.

At first Jane was **nervous** about reading, but she met Abe every day. And they read together. As a result, Jane was learning to read. And she started to like it. One afternoon, Abe surprised her. He gave Jane his **favorite** book about George Washington.

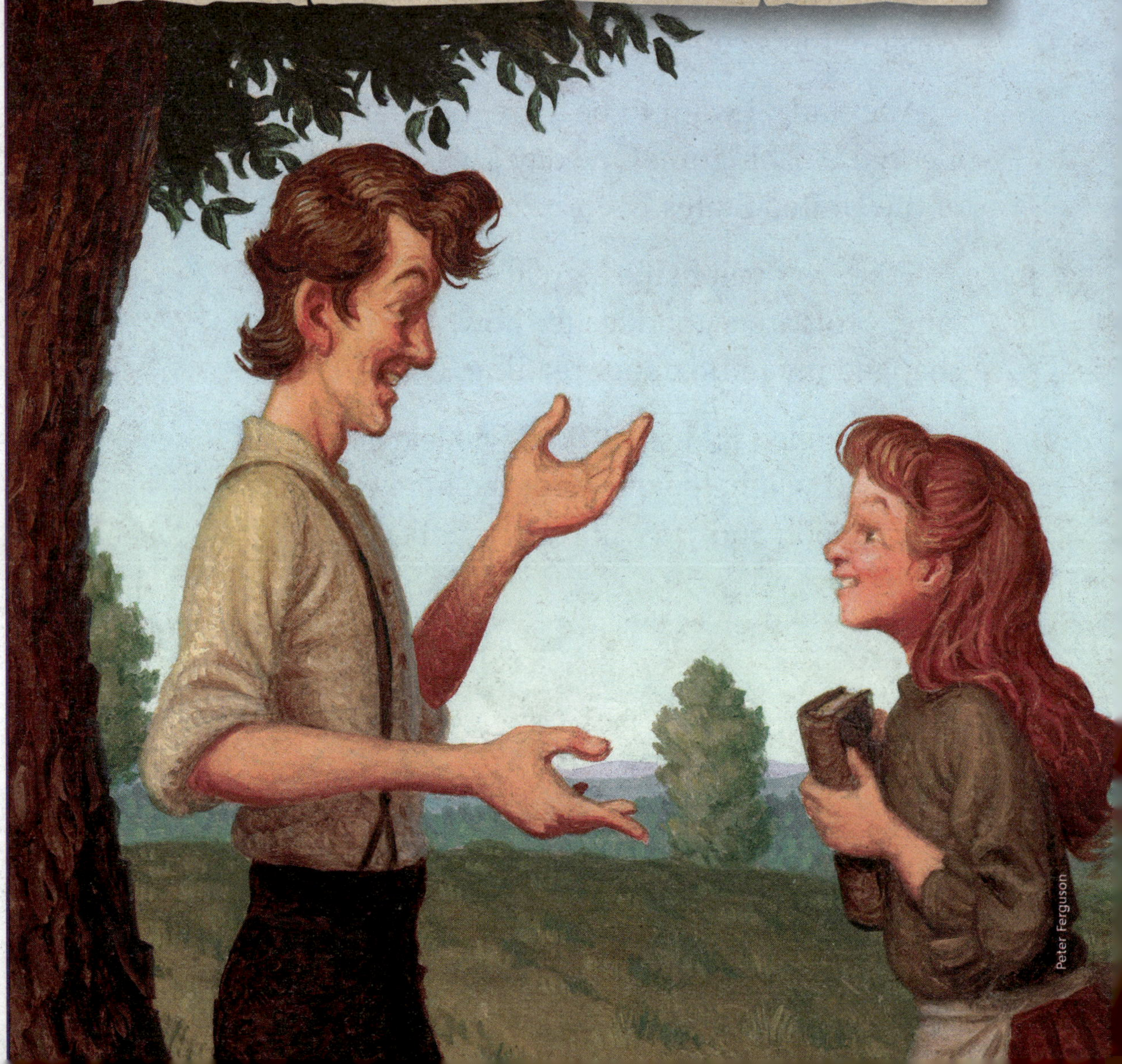

Peter Ferguson

"Thank you," said Jane. "Now I can read, and I do not want to stop."

Years later, Jane was reading her **newspaper** and saw good news. Her friend Abe Lincoln was elected president of the United States. Jane smiled and remembered the day she tripped over Abe's legs. That day changed her life.

Make Connections

 How does Abe change Jane's life? **ESSENTIAL QUESTION**

Who has helped change the way you think? **TEXT TO SELF**

Text Evidence

❶ Specific Vocabulary

Look at the compound word *newspaper*. Write the two small words in *newspaper*.

_____

What does Jane read in the newspaper? Underline the words that tell you.

❷ Sentence Structure ACT

Read the first sentence in the second paragraph. When does Jane read her newspaper? Circle the words that tell you.

❸ Talk About It

How does Abe Lincoln change Jane's life? Cite text evidence.

Abe changes Jane's life by _____

_____

_____.

27

Respond to the Text

 **Partner Discussion** Work with a partner. Read the questions about "Jane's Discovery." Show where you found text evidence. Write the page numbers. Then discuss what you learned.

How does Jane feel about learning to read?

At first, Jane does not want to _____. Page(s): _____

Instead, Jane wants to _____ on the farm. Page(s): _____

Jane tells her parents _____ and runs into the Page(s): _____

_____.

Text Evidence

How does Abe change the way Jane feels?

Abe shows Jane a book about _____. Page(s): _____

Then Abe meets Jane and helps her _____. Page(s): _____

Years later, Jane reads _____ and remembers Page(s): _____

how _____ Abe _____.

Text Evidence

 **Group Discussion** Present your answers to the group. Cite text evidence for your ideas. Listen to and discuss the group's opinions.

 **Write** Work with a partner. Look at your notes about "Jane's Discovery." Write your answer to the Essential Question. Use text evidence to support your answer. Use vocabulary words in your writing.

How does Abe change the way Jane thinks?

At first, Jane does not want _____.

Then Jane meets Abe in the _____.

Abe teaches Jane _____.

Years later, Jane reads about _____.

Abe changes Jane's life because _____.

Share Writing Present your writing to the class. Discuss their opinions. Talk about their ideas. Explain why you agree or disagree with their ideas. You can say:

I agree with _____.

That's a good comment, but _____.

Write to Sources

Isabella

Take Notes About the Text I took notes about the story to respond to the prompt: *Think about when Jane reads the newspaper. Write a letter that Jane writes to Abe after she reads the article. Use details from the story.*

pages 22–27

Jane trips over Abe's legs.

↓

Jane tells Abe she does not want to learn to read.

↓

Abe helps Jane learn to read.

↓

Jane reads in a newspaper that Abe was elected president.

Write About the Text I used notes from my chart to write a letter that Jane writes to Abe.

Student Model: *Narrative Text*

Dear Abe,

  I am happy because you are the president of the United States. I read it in the newspaper.

  I remember the day we met. I tripped over your legs. Your legs were long. Then you helped me to read. It changed my life!

  Your friend,

  Jane

TALK ABOUT IT

Text Evidence
Draw a box around a sentence that comes from the notes. Why does Isabella use this detail in her story?

Grammar
Draw a box around the verb *tripped*. Why does Isabella use past tense here?

Condense Ideas
Circle the sentences about Abe's legs. How can you condense them?

Your Turn

Write a letter from Abe to a friend. Have Abe talk about Jane. Use details from the story.

>> *Go Digital*
Write your response online. Use your editing checklist.

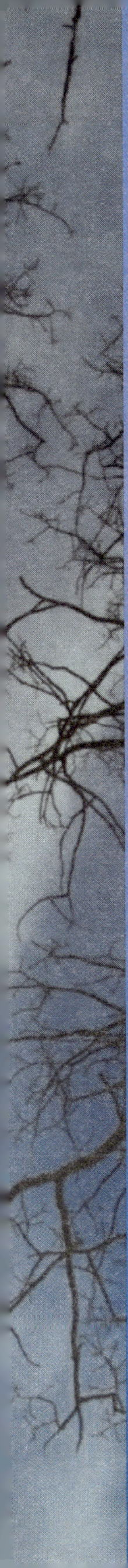

 **What objects are in the sky?** Write those objects in the idea web. Talk about when you see the object. Do you see it in the day or at night?

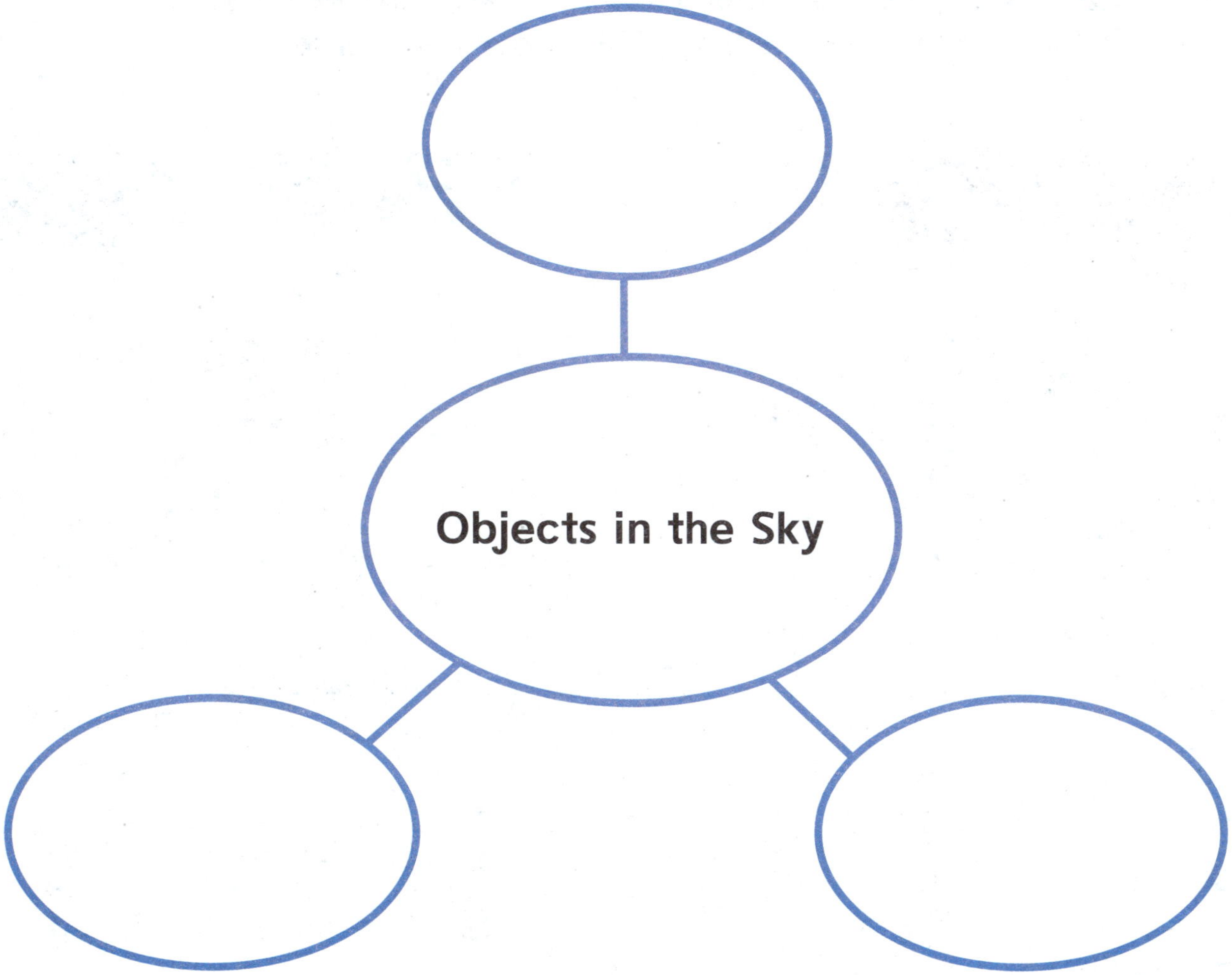

Objects in the Sky

Discuss how close to Earth the objects are. Use the words from the chart. Complete the sentences.

The _____ are close to Earth.

The _____ is far from Earth.

33

More Vocabulary

 Look at the picture and read the word. Then read the sentences. Talk about the word with a partner. Write your own sentence.

collected

Ben **collected** shells.

What word means the same as *collected*?

got   **washed**   **cleaned**

What do you collect?

I collect _____

_____.

discovered

Lane **discovered** an insect in her backyard.

What word means the same as *discovered*?

dug   **hid**   **found**

What is something that you discovered?

I discovered _____

_____.

Words and Phrases: Possessive Nouns and Plurals

Add 's to make a noun possessive.

girl's = belongs to the girl

The **girl's** puppy is cute.

Add *s* to make a noun plural.

girls = more than one girl

I see two **girls**.

 Talk with a partner. Look at the pictures. Read the sentences. Write the word that completes the sentence.

The _____ coat is warm.

boy's   boys

The two _____ play on the swing.

boy's   boys

35

Text Evidence

Shared Read | Genre • Expository

1 Talk About It

Look at the picture. Read the title. Discuss what you see. Use these words.

**telescope   Earth   Moon
sky   neighbors**

Write about what you see.

What is the man doing?

The man is looking through ____
_____.

What does the man see?

The man sees _____
_____.

What is the text about?

The text is about _____
_____.

Take notes as you read the text.

Earth and Its Neighbors

Essential Question

What do we know about Earth and its neighbors?

Read about how we learn about space.

This is Galileo. He studied the sky with a telescope.